The Prophet Described

My First Meeting With Muhammad ﷺ

"The Messenger of Allah ﷺ was more handsome, more beautiful and more radiant than the full moon."

From the words of Jābir Ibn 'Abdillah ﷺ describing the Prophet Muhammad ﷺ

First published in the United Kingdom in 1441 AH (2021 CE) by
Learning Roots Ltd.
Unit 6, TGEC, Town Hall Approach Road, London, N15 4RX
www.learningroots.com

Copyright © Learning Roots 2021
Authored by Zaheer Khatri.
Illustrations, layout and design by Fatima Zahur, Elaine Lim and Jannah Haque.

Acknowledgements
The publisher thanks Allah, Lord of the Worlds, for making this publication possible.

British Library Cataloguing in Publication Data
A CIP catalogue record for this book is available from the British Library.

Printed and bound by in Turkey.
ISBN: 978-1-915381-00-2

إِنْ صَمَتَ فَعَلَيهِ الوَقَارُ،
وإِنْ تَكَلَّمَ سَمَا وعَلَاهُ البَهَاءُ،
أَجمَلُ النَّاسِ وأَبهَاهُ مِن بَعِيدٍ،
وَأَحْلَاهُ وأَحْسَنهُ مِن قَرِيبٍ

When he was silent, he was dignified.
When he spoke, he was eminent, magnificent.
He was the most striking and beautiful
of people when seen from afar,
and the finest and best of them
when seen up close.

*From the description of Umm Ma'bad ☺, a Bedouin woman
who met the Prophet ﷺ on his famous migration
journey (hijrah) from Makkah to Madinah.*

"Zayd, my son," said Mummy,
"One day you'll meet a special man,
The finest soul you'll ever see.
The more you get to know him,
The greater your love will be."

"Ma-sha-Allah!" said Zayd.
"Please describe him to me.
Tell me all about him,
So I can guess who he could be."

2

"He was the most handsome man,
More beautiful than the full moon.
You'd cherish every moment with him
And wish your meeting would come soon.

"He'd embrace you with a smiling face,
So cheerful and so bright,
Greeting you with words of peace,
Guiding you towards light."

"Amazing!" said Zayd.
"How gracious that man must be!
Please continue, Mummy.
Describe him more to me."

"His fragrance was so sweet,
Radiating from his sweat,
A scent finer than musk,
Embracing you long before you'd met.

"As you'd address him,
His attention would be all yours.
He'd make you feel so special,
Facing you like open shores."

"Incredible!" said Zayd.
"How thoughtful that man must be!
Please carry on, Mummy.
Describe him more to me."

"He'd extend his hand for you to shake,
So the love between you would grow.
He'd keep hold of your hand,
Until you would let his go.

"His palms were softer than silk;
You'd never feel a more comfy touch.
He'd cater to your subtle feelings,
His care and attention were such."

"Lovely!" said Zayd.
"How comforting that man must be!
What else can you tell me, Mummy?
Describe him more to me."

8

"His every word was like a gem,
Full of meaning, so measured and grand.
From each one, wisdom would stem,
Spoken clearly for you to understand.

"He'd elevate blessings around him,
And never find faults or complain.
His outlook on life was exquisite,
Beyond what words could explain."

"Astounding!" said Zayd.
"How positive that man must be!
Please keep going, Mummy.
Describe him more to me."

"He was neither tall nor short,
Rather a little more than medium in height.
His complexion was neither dark nor light,
And his skin glowed elegantly bright.

"His hair was neither curly nor straight,
 But flowed to his shoulders in waves,
 Obeying if he parted it,
 Rich black for most of his days."

"Marvellous!" said Zayd.
"How perfect that man must be!
 Don't stop there, Mummy.
 Describe him more to me."

"His eyelashes extended long
  Below eyebrows, finely haired.
  His eyes held a powerful gaze
  With dark pupils that seldom stared.

"His mouth stretched wide,
  Housing teeth that were fine and bright,
  Arranged with slender spaces,
  As if between them would emanate a light."

"Charming!" said Zayd.
"How handsome that man must be!
Your words delight me, Mummy.
Describe him more to me."

14

"Poised upon his silvery-clear neck,
Was his large and flawless head.
His nose had a gentle bridge,
And his beard was densely spread.

"His forearms were long and strong;
His chest and stomach were aligned.
His hands and feet were fully fleshed,
And all were smoothly refined."

"Wonderful!" said Zayd.
"How strong that man must be!
Please proceed, Mummy.
Describe him more to me."

"He walked softly with purpose,
Well-paced as if descending downhill.
You'd hardly keep up with him,
Such was his energy and will.

17

"His shoulders spread out broad.
 Pressed between them was a seal,
 A blend of raised skin and hair:
 A sign of his Prophethood for real."

"Extraordinary!" said Zayd.
"How blessed that man must be!
 I don't want this to end, Mummy.
 Describe him more to me."

18

"It was as if time stood still for him;
Handling pressure with patience of steel.
With an unshakable trust in his Lord,
Countless hearts did he heal.

"His bravery was unmatched,
With a mission-focus so sincere;
Relentless no matter the challenge,
And only Allah did he fear."

"Remarkable!" said Zayd.
"How confident that man must be!
I'm so impressed, Mummy.
Describe him more to me."

20

"If you were ever missing,
    He'd notice and ask about you.
    His sincerity would melt your heart,
    With love that always held true.

"While everyone in his lofty class
    Has used up their special prayer,
    He reserved his wish just for you
    To comfort you on a day of fear."

21

"Subhan-Allah!" said Zayd.
"How loving that man must be!
I wish to be with him, Mummy.
Describe him more to me."

22

"There's never been the likes of him,
Neither before nor after his time,
Chosen especially by Allah,
Fashioned incredibly sublime.

"He had the most graceful manners;
You'll never find character so refined.
He had every good in him,
Sent as a mercy to mankind.

"My description has not done him justice,
But can you guess who he could be?"

"There's only one man," said Zayd,
"Whose beauty reaches so far.
He must be...

26

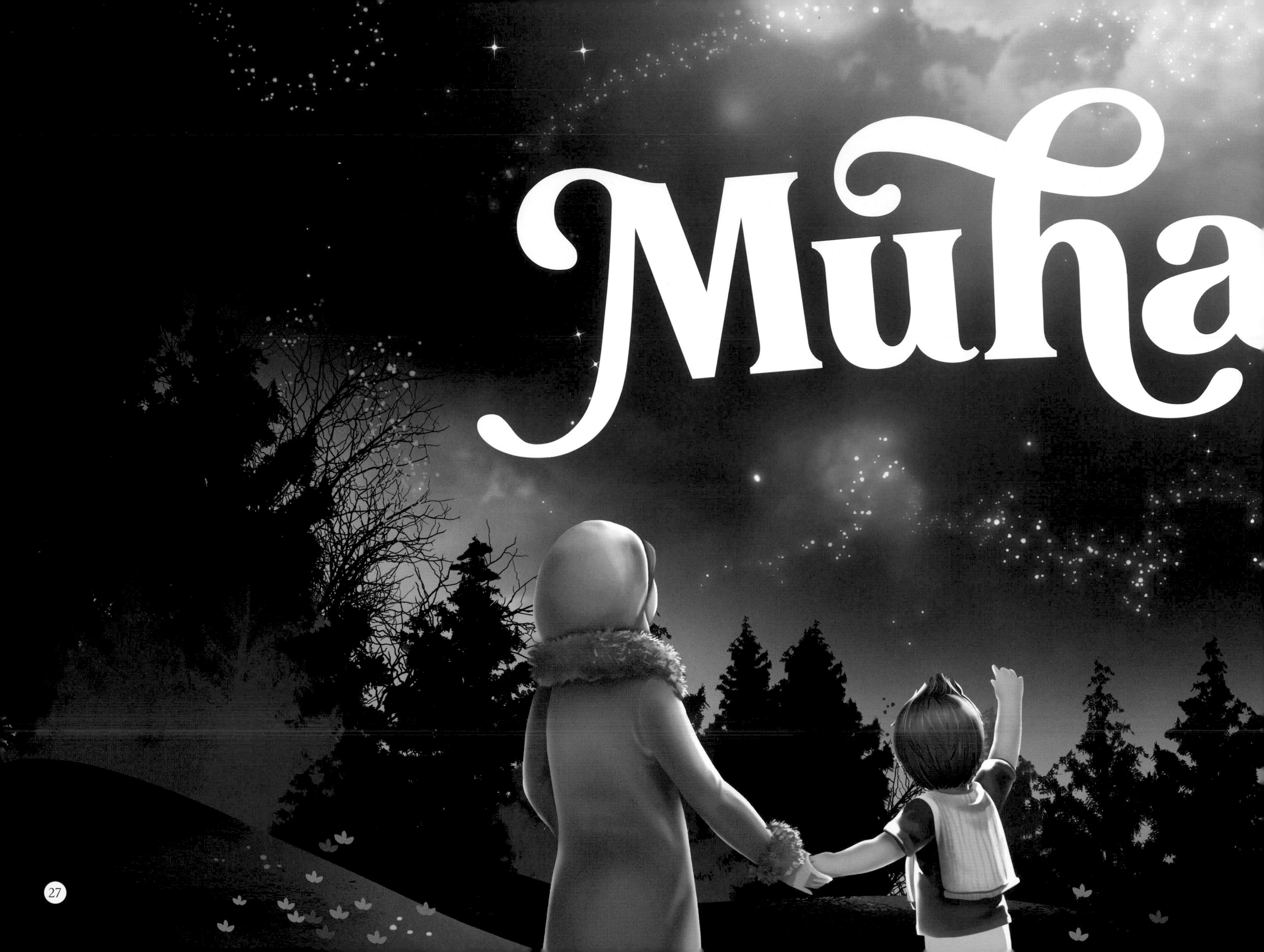
Muha

mmad ﷺ

The Messenger of Allah.

"Yes, indeed," said Mummy.
"We'll meet him on the Last Day.
Just before we enter Jannah,
If we follow him on his way."

"We'll do our best," said Zayd,
"To follow his wonderful way.
But where will we find him, Mummy?
It will be so crowded on that day."

"We'll find him by a special pond,
Whose description is so sublime.
Together, we'll learn about it,
But that'll be for another time..."

30

أَوْلَى النَّاسِ بِي يَوْمَ القِيَامَةِ أَكْثَرُهُم عَلَيَّ صَلَاةً

Ibn Mas'ud ⬦ reported that the Messenger of Allah ⬦ said,

"The people who will be nearest to me
on the Day of Resurrection will be those who
supplicate to Allah most often for me."

Abu Dawud, Tirmidhi & Ibn Hibban

May the peace and blessings of Allah
be upon Muhammad.

"You'll find him by a special pond,
Whose description is so sublime.
Together, we'll learn about it,
But that'll be for another time..."

Continue the journey with Zayd and Mummy and discover your meeting place with the Prophet Muhammad ﷺ

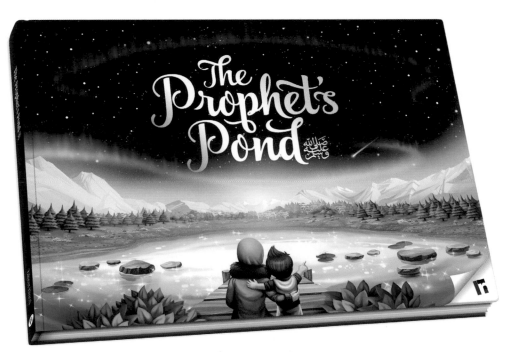

To get your copy, visit

Learning Roots.com

Describing the Prophet Muhammad ﷺ

How would you describe the face of the Messenger of Allah ﷺ?

How would you describe the body of the Prophet Muhammad ﷺ?

How would you describe the speech of the Messenger of Allah ﷺ?

How would you describe the manner in which the Prophet Muhammad ﷺ would greet people?

How would you describe the hair of the Messenger of Allah ﷺ?

How would you describe the walk of the Prophet Muhammad ﷺ?

Loving the Prophet Muhammad ﷺ

How would you describe the character of the Prophet Muhammad ﷺ?

How would you describe the love that the Prophet Muhammad ﷺ has for you?

Describe how it would feel to be in the company of the Prophet Muhammad ﷺ.

What must you do to be in the company of the Prophet Muhammad ﷺ in the hereafter?

Story Reference Index
Please see the matching reference numbers on the pages that follow.

"He was the most handsome man, (2)

More beautiful than the full moon. (14)

You'd cherish every moment with him (26)

And wish your meeting would come soon. (26)

"He'd embrace you with a smiling face, (11)

So cheerful and so bright, (25)

Greeting you with words of peace, (24)

Guiding you towards light. (33)

"His fragrance was so sweet, (15)

Radiating from his sweat, (20)

A scent finer than musk, (15)

Embracing you long before you'd met.

"As you'd address him,

His attention would be all yours. (17)

He'd make you feel so special,

Facing you like open shores. (17)

"He'd extend his hand for you to shake, (18)

So the love between you would grow.

He'd keep hold of your hand, (16)

Until you would let his go. (16)

"His palms were softer than silk. (15)

You'd never feel a more comfy touch. (15)

He'd cater to your subtle feelings, (4)

His care and attention were such. (4)

"His every word was like a gem, (10)

Full of meaning, so measured and grand. (10)

From each one, wisdom would stem, (10)

Spoken clearly for you to understand. (9)

"He'd elevate blessings around him, (31)

And never find faults or complain, (15)

His outlook on life was exquisite, (19)

Beyond what words could explain. (19)

"He was neither tall nor short, (1)

Rather a little more than medium in height. (1)

His complexion was neither dark nor light, (1)

And his skin glowed elegantly bright. (25)

"His hair was neither curly nor straight, (1)

But flowed to his shoulders in waves, (1)

Obeying if he parted it, (24)

Rich black for most of his days. (1)

"His eyelashes extended long (17)

Below eyebrows, finely haired; (24)

His eyes held a powerful gaze (24)

With dark pupils that seldom stared. (24)

"His mouth stretched wide, (21)

Housing teeth that were fine and bright, (12)

Arranged with slender spaces, (12)

As if between them would emanate a light. (12)

"Poised upon his silvery-clear neck, (24)

Was his large and flawless head. (3) (17)

His nose had a gentle bridge, (24)

And his beard was densely spread. (17)

"His forearms were long and strong. (24)

His chest and stomach were aligned. (24)

His hands and feet were fully fleshed, (3) (17)

And all were smoothly refined. (13)

"He walked softly with purpose, (25)

Well-paced as if descending downhill. (3)

You'd hardly keep up with him, (25)

Such was his energy and will.

"His shoulders spread out broad. (2)
Pressed between them was a seal, (22) (23)
A blend of raised skin and hair: (22) (23)
A sign of his Prophethood for real. (23)

"It was as if time stood still for him,
Handling pressure with patience of steel. (32)
With an unshakable trust in his Lord, (4)
Countless hearts did he heal. (33)

"His bravery was unmatched, (8)
With a mission-focus so sincere. (30)
Relentless no matter the challenge,
And only Allah did he fear.

"And if you were ever missing, (7)
He'd notice and ask about you. (7)
His sincerity would melt your heart,
With love that always held true. (27)

"While everyone in his lofty class (6)
Has used up their special prayer, (6)
He reserved his wish just for you (6)
To comfort you on a day of fear. (6)

"There's never been the likes of him, (3)
Neither before nor after his time, (3)
Chosen especially by Allah, (28)
Fashioned incredibly sublime. (4)

"He had the most graceful manners; (4)
You'll never find a character so refined. (4)
He had every good in him, (4)
Sent as a mercy to mankind. (5)

"My description has not done him justice,
But can you guess who he could be?"

"There's only one man," said Zayd,
"Whose beauty reaches so far.
He must be...

"Muhammad ﷺ
The Messenger of Allah." (28)

"Yes, indeed," said Mummy.
"We'll meet him on the Last Day.
Just before we enter Jannah,
If we follow him on his way."

"We'll do our best," said Zayd,
"To follow his wonderful way.
But where will we find him, Mummy?
It will be so crowded on that day."

"You'll find him by a special pond, (29)
Whose description is so sublime.
Together, we'll learn about it,
But that'll be for another time..."

References

1

عَنْ أَنَسِ بْنِ مَالِكٍ ﷺ: كَانَ رَسُولُ اللَّهِ ﷺ لَيْسَ بِالطَّوِيلِ الْبَائِنِ، وَلَا بِالْقَصِيرِ، وَلَيْسَ بِالْأَبْيَضِ الْأَمْهَقِ، وَلَيْسَ بِالآدَمِ، وَلَيْسَ بِالْجَعْدِ الْقَطَطِ، وَلَا بِالسَّبْطِ، بَعَثَهُ اللَّهُ عَلَى رَأْسِ أَرْبَعِينَ سَنَةً، فَأَقَامَ بِمَكَّةَ عَشْرَ سِنِينَ، وَبِالْمَدِينَةِ عَشْرَ سِنِينَ، وَتَوَفَّاهُ اللَّهُ عَلَى رَأْسِ سِتِّينَ سَنَةً، وَلَيْسَ فِي رَأْسِهِ وَلِحْيَتِهِ عِشْرُونَ شَعَرَةً بَيْضَاءَ

Narrated Anas bin Mālik ﷺ: "The Prophet ﷺ was neither conspicuously tall nor conspicuously short; neither very light nor very dark. His hair was neither very curled nor very straight. Allah sent him (as a Prophet) at the age of forty; and after that, he stayed for ten years in Mecca and for ten more years in Madinah. Allah took him unto Him at the age of sixty, and he scarcely had ten white hairs on his head and in his beard."

Sahih Al-Bukhari

2

عَنِ الْبَرَاءِ ﷺ قَالَ: مَا رَأَيْتُ مِنْ ذِي لِمَّةٍ أَحْسَنَ فِي حُلَّةٍ حَمْرَاءَ مِنْ رَسُولِ اللَّهِ ﷺ شَعْرُهُ يَضْرِبُ مَنْكِبَيْهِ بَعِيدَ مَا بَيْنَ الْمَنْكِبَيْنِ لَيْسَ بِالطَّوِيلِ وَلَا بِالْقَصِيرِ

Al-Barā bin Aazib ﷺ reported: "Never have I seen anyone more handsome than Allah's Messenger ﷺ in a red mantle. His hair hung down to his shoulders, and his shoulders were very broad. He was neither very tall nor short-statured."

Sahih Muslim

3

عَنْ عَلِيِّ بْنِ أَبِي طَالِبٍ ﷺ قَالَ: لَمْ يَكُنِ النبي ﷺ بِالطَّوِيلِ وَلَا بِالْقَصِيرِ شَثْنُ الْكَفَّيْنِ وَالْقَدَمَيْنِ ضَخْمُ الرَّأْسِ ضَخْمُ الْكَرَادِيسِ طَوِيلُ الْمَسْرُبَةِ إِذَا مَشَى تَكَفَّأَ تَكَفُّؤًا كَأَنَّمَا يَنْحَطُّ مِنْ صَبَبٍ لَمْ أَرَ قَبْلَهُ وَلَا بعده مثله ﷺ

'Ali Ibn Abi Tālib ﷺ reported: "The Messenger of Allah ﷺ was neither very tall nor very short. The soles of his feet were fully-fleshed. He had a large head. The joints of his bones were large. A thin line of hair ran from his chest to his navel. When The Messenger of Allah ﷺ walked, it appeared as though he were descending from a high place. I have not seen anyone like him, neither before nor after him."

At-Tirmidhi in Ash-Shama'il Al-Muhammadiyyah, graded Sound by Al-Albani

4

وَإِنَّكَ لَعَلَى خُلُقٍ عَظِيمٍ

And you (O Prophet) are truly of outstanding character.

The Noble Quran, Surah 68, Al-Qalam, Verse 4

5

وَمَا أَرْسَلْنَاكَ إِلَّا رَحْمَةً لِّلْعَلَمِينَ

And We have not sent you, (O Prophet), but as a mercy to the whole world.

The Noble Quran, Surah 21, Al-Anbiyaa', Verse 107

6

عَنْ أَبِي هُرَيْرَةَ ﷺ قَالَ: قَالَ رَسُولُ الله ﷺ: لِكل نَبِي دَعْوَة مُسْتَجَابَة، فَتَعَجل كل نَبِي دَعْوَتَه، وَإِني اخْتَبَأْتُ دَعْوَتِي، شَفَاعَة لِأُمتِي يَوم الْقِيَامَة، فَهِي نَائِلَة إِن شَاءَ الله مَن مَاتَ مِن أُمتِي لَا يُشْرِكُ بِالله شَيْئا

Abu Hurayrah ﷺ reported that The Messenger of Allah ﷺ said: "Every Prophet has a granted prayer, but every prophet has used his prayer. I have, however, reserved my prayer for the intercession of

my *Ummah* on the Day of Judgement. And it will be granted, if Allah wills, for whoever dies among my *Ummah* not having associated anything with Allah."
Sahih Muslim

عَن هِندِ بنِ أَبِي هَالَة ﷺ أَنَّ رَسُولَ اللَّهِ ﷺ كَانَ يَتَفَقَّدُ أَصْحَابَه، وَيَسْأَلُ النَّاسَ عَمَّا فِي النَّاسِ

Hind Ibn Abi Hala ﷺ reported that the Messenger of Allah ﷺ would inquire about the whereabouts of his Companions (if they were missing) and would ask the people about their condition.
At-Tabarani in Al-Kabir and Al-Bayhaqi in Ash-Su'b who said this hadith contained indicators of its acceptability. Others have graded this hadith as Weak.

عَنْ أَنَسِ بْنِ مَالِكٍ ﷺ قَالَ كَانَ رَسُولُ اللَّهِ ﷺ أَحْسَنَ النَّاسِ وَكَانَ أَجْوَدَ النَّاسِ وَكَانَ أَشْجَعَ النَّاسِ وَلَقَدْ فَزِعَ أَهْلُ الْمَدِينَةِ ذَاتَ لَيْلَةٍ فَانْطَلَقَ نَاسٌ قِبَلَ الصَّوْتِ فَتَلَقَّاهُمْ رَسُولُ اللَّهِ ﷺ رَاجِعًا وَقَدْ سَبَقَهُمْ إِلَى الصَّوْتِ وَهُوَ عَلَى فَرَسٍ لِأَبِي طَلْحَةَ عُرْيٍ فِي عُنُقِهِ السَّيْفُ وَهُوَ يَقُولُ: لَمْ تُرَاعُوا لَمْ تُرَاعُوا , قَالَ: وَجَدْنَاهُ بَحْرًا أَوْ إِنَّهُ لَبَحْرٌ , قَالَ: وَكَانَ فَرَسًا يُبَطَّأُ

Anas Ibn Malik ﷺ said: "Among all the people, Allah's Messenger ﷺ had the most sublime character; he was the most generous and bravest of men. One night, the people of Madinah were disturbed by a loud sound and set forth to investigate. Allah's Messenger ﷺ had gone towards the sound ahead of them and met them on his way back. He was on Abu Talha's horse and used no saddle; a sword hung from a strap around his neck, and he said: 'There is nothing to be afraid of,' and 'We found this horse like a torrent of water,' meaning that the horse was fast, though it had been slow before that time."
Sahih Muslim

عَنْ عَائِشَة ﷺ قَالَتْ: مَا كَانَ رَسُولُ الله ﷺ يَسْرُدُ كَسَرْدِكم هَذَا وَلَكِنَّهُ كَانَ يَتَكَلَّمُ بِكَلَامٍ بَيِّنٍ فَصْلٍ يَحْفَظُهُ من جَلَسَ إِلَيْهِ

'Aisha ﷺ said: "The Messenger of Allah ﷺ did not speak quickly like you do now; rather, he would speak so clearly and unmistakably that those who sat with him would memorize it."
At-Tirmidhi in Ash-Shama'il Al-Muhammadiyyah, graded Authentic by Al-Albani

حَدَّثَنَا أَبُو هُرَيْرَة ﷺ عَنْ رَسُولِ اللَّهِ ﷺ فَذَكَرَ أَحَادِيثَ مِنْهَا: قَالَ رَسُولُ اللَّهِ ﷺ: نُصِرْتُ بِالرُّعْبِ وَأُوتِيتُ جَوَامِعَ الْكَلِمِ

Abu Hurayrah ﷺ reported that the Messenger of Allah ﷺ said: "I have been helped by dread (in the hearts of enemies) and I have been given words which are concise yet comprehensive in meaning."
Sahih Muslim

References

11

عَنْ عَبْدِ اللَّهِ بْنِ الْحَارِثِ بْنِ جَزْءٍ ﷺ قَالَ مَا رَأَيْتُ أَحَدًا أَكْثَرَ تَبَسُّمًا مِنْ رَسُولِ اللَّهِ ﷺ

'Abdullah Ibn Harith Ibn Jaz ﷺ said, "I have not seen anyone who smiled more than The Messenger of Allah ﷺ."

At-Tirmidhi in Ash-Shama'il Al-Muhammadiyyah, graded Authentic by Al-Albani

12

عَنْ عَبْدِ اللَّهِ بْنِ عَبَّاسٍ ﷺ قَالَ : كَانَ رَسُولَ اللَّهِ ﷺ أَفْلَجَ الثَّنِيَّتَيْنِ، إِذَا تَكَلَّمَ رُؤِيَ كَالنورِ يَخْرُجُ مِنْ بَيْنِ ثَنَايَاهُ

'Abdullah Ibn Abbas ﷺ said: "The Messenger of Allah ﷺ's front teeth were spaced out and not close together. When he spoke, those around him could see illumination emitting from between his front teeth.

As-Suyuti in Al-Jami' As-Sagheer, graded Authentic by At-Tabarani

13

عَنْ أَبِي هُرَيْرَةَ ﷺ قَالَ : كَانَ رَسُولَ اللَّهِ ﷺ أَبْيَضَ كَأَنَّمَا صِيغَ مِنْ فِضَّةٍ رَجِلَ الشَّعْرِ

Abu Hurayrah ﷺ said: "The Messenger of Allah ﷺ was so clean and clear, as though his body were moulded from silver. His hair was neither curly nor straight."

At-Tirmidhi in Ash-Shama'il Al-Muhammadiyyah, graded Authentic by Al-Albani

14

قَالَ جَابِرَ بْنَ سَمُرَةَ ﷺ رَأَيْتُ رَسُولَ اللَّهِ ﷺ فِي لَيْلَةِ إِضْحِيَان (مضيئة مقمرة) وَعَلَيْهِ حُلَّةٌ حَمْرَاءُ فَجَعَلْتُ أَنْظُرُ إِلَيْهِ وَإِلَى الْقَمَرِ فَلَهُوَ عِنْدِي أَحْسَنُ مِنَ القمر

Narrated Jabir ﷺ: "I once saw The Messenger of Allah ﷺ on the night of a full moon. On that night he wore red clothing. At times, I looked at the full moon, and at times, at The Messenger of Allah ﷺ. Ultimately, I concluded that The Messenger of Allah ﷺ was more handsome, more beautiful and more radiant than the full moon."

At-Tirmidhi in Ash-Shama'il Al-Muhammadiyyah, graded Authentic by Al-Albani

15

عَنْ أَنَسِ بْنِ مَالِكٍ ﷺ قَالَ: مَا مَسِسْتُ دِيبَاجاً وَلاَ حَرِيراً أَلْيَنَ مِنْ كَفِّ رَسُولِ الله ﷺ، وَلاَ شَمَمْتُ رَائِحَةً قَطُّ أَطْيَبَ مِنْ رَائِحَةِ رسولِ الله ﷺ، وَلَقَدْ خدمتُ رسول الله ﷺ عَشْرَ سنين، فما قَالَ لِي قَطُّ: أُفٍّ، وَلاَ قَالَ لِشَيءٍ فَعَلْتُهُ: لِمَ فَعَلْتهُ، وَلاَ لشَيءٍ لَمْ أَفْعَله: أَلاَ فَعَلْتَ كَذا؟

Anas bin Malik ﷺ reported: "I have never touched plain or woven silk softer than the palm of The Messenger of Allah ﷺ, nor have I smelt a perfume more pleasant than the scent of The Messenger of Allah ﷺ. Indeed, I have served The Messenger of Allah for ten years, and not once did he say 'uff' to me. He never asked, 'Why did you do it?' about something I had done or 'Why didn't you do it?' about something I hadn't done."

Sahih Al-Bukhari & Sahih Muslim

عَنْ أَنَسِ بْنِ مَالِكٍ ﷺ قَالَ: كَانَ النَّبِيُّ ﷺ إِذَا لَقِيَهُ أَحَدٌ مِنْ أَصْحَابِهِ فَقَامَ مَعَهُ ، قَامَ مَعَهُ فَلَمْ يَنْصَرِفْ حَتَّى يَكُونَ الرَّجُلُ هُوَ الَّذِي يَنْصَرِفُ عَنْهُ ، وَإِذَا لَقِيَهُ أَحَدٌ مِنْ أَصْحَابِهِ فَتَنَاوَلَ يَدَهُ نَاوَلَهُ إِيَّاهَا فَلَمْ يَنْزِعْ يَدَهُ مِنْهُ حَتَّى يَكُونَ الرَّجُلُ هُوَ الَّذِي يَنْزِعُ يَدَهُ مِنْهُ ، وَإِذَا لَقِيَ أَحَدًا مِنْ أَصْحَابِهِ فَتَنَاوَلَ أُذُنَهُ ، نَاوَلَهُ إِيَّاهَا ، ثُمَّ لَمْ يَنْزِعْهَا حَتَّى يَكُونَ الرَّجُلُ هُوَ الَّذِي يَنْزِعُهَا عَنْهُ

Anas bin Malik ﷺ narrated: "When the Prophet ﷺ would meet one of his Companions, he would stay with him until the Companion left himself. And when the Prophet ﷺ would receive one of his Companions, he would shake hands with him and would not remove his hand until the Companion removed his. And when the Prophet ﷺ would receive one of his Companions, he would listen to him until the Companion had finished.

Ibn Sa'd in At-Tabaqat Al-Kubra, graded Authentic by Al-Albani in Sahih Al-Jami'

عَنْ مُحَمَّدِ بْنِ عَلِيٍّ، رَضِيَ اللَّهُ عَنْهُ عَنْ أَبِيهِ، قَالَ كَانَ رَسُولُ اللَّهِ ﷺ ضَخْمَ الرَّأْسِ عَظِيمَ الْعَيْنَيْنِ هَدِبَ الْأَشْفَارِ مُشْرَبَ الْعَيْنِ بِحُمْرَةٍ كَثَّ اللِّحْيَةِ أَزْهَرَ اللَّوْنِ إِذَا مَشَى تَكَفَّأَ كَأَنَّمَا يَمْشِي فِي صُعُدٍ وَإِذَا الْتَفَتَ الْتَفَتَ جَمِيعًا شَثْنَ الْكَفَّيْنِ وَالْقَدَمَيْنِ

Muhammad Ibn 'Ali narrated that his father said: "The Messenger of Allah ﷺ had a large head, big eyes, long eyelashes, a touch of red in his eyes, a thick beard and a pinkish colour. When he walked, he leaned forward as though walking uphill. When he turned, he turned with his whole body. He had large hands and feet.

Ahmed in Al-Musnad, graded Authentic by Ahmed Shakir

عَنْ أَبِي هُرَيْرَةَ ﷺ قَالَ: قَالَ رَسُولُ اللَّهِ ﷺ إِنَّ الْمُسْلِمَ إِذَا صَافَحَ أَخَاهُ تَحَاتَّتْ خَطَايَاهُمَا كَمَا يَتَحَاتُّ وَرَقُ الشَّجَرِ

Abu Hurayrah ﷺ reported that The Messenger of Allah ﷺ said, "Indeed, when a Muslim shakes hands with his brother, both of their sins fall away like leaves falling from a tree."

Musnad Al-Bazzār, Authentic through corroborating evidence

عن قتادة قُلْتُ يَا أُمَّ الْمُؤْمِنِينَ (عائشة) أَنْبِئِينِي عَنْ خُلُقِ رَسُولِ اللَّهِ ﷺ قَالَتْ أَلَسْتَ تَقْرَأُ الْقُرْآنَ قُلْتُ بَلَى قَالَتْ فَإِنَّ خُلُقَ نَبِيِّ اللَّهِ ﷺ كَانَ الْقُرْآنَ

Qatadah reported: "I said to 'Aisha ﷺ, 'O mother of the Believers, tell me about the character of the Messenger of Allah ﷺ.' 'Aisha ﷺ said, 'Have you not read the Quran?' I said, 'Of course.' 'Aisha ﷺ said, 'Indeed, the character of the Prophet of Allah ﷺ was the Quran.'"

Sahih Muslim

References

20

عَنْ أَبِي أَنَسِ بْنِ مَالِكٍ ﷺ قَالَ دَخَلَ عَلَيْنَا النَّبِيُّ ﷺ فَقَامَ عِنْدَنَا فَعَرِقَ وَجَاءَتْ أُمِّي بِقَارُورَةٍ فَجَعَلَتْ تَسْلُتُ الْعَرَقَ فِيهَا فَاسْتَيْقَظَ النَّبِيُّ ﷺ فَقَالَ: يَا أُمَّ سُلَيْمٍ مَا هَذَا الَّذِي تَصْنَعِينَ, قَالَتْ هَذَا عَرَقُكَ نَجْعَلُهُ فِي طِيبِنَا وَهُوَ مِنْ أَطْيَبِ الطِّيبِ

Anas Ibn Malik ﷺ reported: "Allah's Messenger ﷺ would stay at my house and there was perspiration upon his body. My mother brought a bottle and began to pour the sweat into it. When Allah's Messenger ﷺ woke up, he said: 'Umm Sulaim, what are doing?' She said: 'It's your sweat. We mix it with our perfume and it becomes the most fragrant scent.'"

Sahih Muslim

21

جَابِرِ بْنِ سَمُرَةَ يَقُولُ: كَانَ رَسُولُ اللَّهِ ﷺ ضَلِيعَ الْفَمِ أَشْكَلَ الْعَيْنِ مَنْهُوسَ الْعَقِبِ

Jābir Ibn Samurah ﷺ said: "The Messenger of Allah ﷺ had a wide mouth. There were red lines in the whiteness of his eyes. He had little flesh on his heels."

At-Tirmidhi in Ash-Shama'il Al-Muhammadiyyah, graded Authentic by Al-Albani

22

أَبُو زَيْدٍ عَمْرُو بْنُ أَخْطَبَ الْأَنْصَارِيُّ ﷺ قَالَ: قَالَ لِي رَسُولُ اللَّهِ ﷺ: يَا أَبَا زَيْدٍ ادْنُ مِنِّي فَامْسَحْ ظَهْرِي, فَمَسَحْتُ ظَهْرَهُ فَوَقَعَتْ أَصَابِعِي عَلَى الْخَاتَمِ. قُلْتُ: وَمَا الْخَاتَمُ. قال: شعرات مُجْتَمِعَات

Abu Zayd 'Amr bin Akhtab Al-Ansāri ﷺ narrated: "The Messenger of Allah ﷺ once said to me, 'O Abu Zayd! Come and massage my back.' When I began massaging his back, my fingers touched the Seal of Prophethood." 'Amr ﷺ was asked, "What is the Seal of Prophethood?" He replied: "It was a collection of a few hairs."

At-Tirmidhi in Ash-Shama'il Al-Muhammadiyyah, graded Authentic by Al-Albani

23

عَنْ أَبِي نَضْرَةَ الْعَوْفِي قَالَ: سَأَلْتُ أَبَا سَعِيدٍ الْخُدْرِيَّ عَنْ خَاتَمِ رَسُولِ الله ﷺ, يَعْنِي خَاتَمَ النُّبُوَّةِ فَقَالَ: كَانَ فِي ظَهْرِهِ بَضْعَةٌ نَاشِزَةٌ

Abi Nadrah Al-'Awfee ﷺ reported: "I asked Abu Sa'eed Al-Khudri ﷺ about the Seal of Prophethood on The Messenger of Allah ﷺ. He said: 'It was a piece of raised flesh that was on The Messenger's ﷺ back.'"

At-Tirmidhi in Ash-Shama'il Al-Muhammadiyyah, graded Sound by Al-Albani

24

عَنِ ابْنِ أَبِي هَالَةَ، عَنِ الْحَسَنِ بْنِ عَلِيٍّ، قَالَ: سَأَلْتُ خَالِي هِنْدَ بْنَ أَبِي هَالَةَ، وَكَانَ وَصَّافًا، عَنْ حِلْيَةِ رَسُولِ الله ﷺ، وَأَنَا أَشْتَهِي أَنْ يَصِفَ لِي مِنْهَا شَيْئًا أَتَعَلَّقُ بِهِ، فَقَالَ: كَانَ رَسُولُ الله ﷺ فَخْمًا مُفَخَّمًا، يَتَلَأْلَأُ وَجْهُهُ، تَلَأْلُؤَ الْقَمَرِ لَيْلَةَ الْبَدْرِ، أَطْوَلَ مِنَ الْمَرْبُوعِ، وَأَقْصَرَ مِنَ الْمُشَذَّبِ، عَظِيمَ الْهَامَةِ، رَجِلَ الشَّعْرِ، إِنِ انْفَرَقَتْ عَقِيقَتُهُ فَرَقَهَا، وَإِلَّا فَلَا يُجَاوِزُ شَعْرُهُ شَحْمَةَ أُذُنَيْهِ، إِذَا هُوَ وَفَّرَهُ، أَزْهَرَ اللَّوْنِ، وَاسِعَ الْجَبِينِ، أَزَجَّ الْحَوَاجِبِ، سَوَابِغَ فِي غَيْرِ قَرَنٍ، بَيْنَهُمَا عِرْقٌ، يُدِرُّهُ الْغَضَبُ، أَقْنَى الْعِرْنَيْنِ، لَهُ نُورٌ يَعْلُوهُ، يَحْسِبُهُ مَنْ لَمْ يَتَأَمَّلْهُ أَشَمَّ، كَثَّ اللِّحْيَةِ، سَهْلَ الْخَدَّيْنِ، ضَلِيعَ الْفَمِ، مُفْلَجَ الْأَسْنَانِ، دَقِيقَ الْمَسْرُبَةِ، كَأَنَّ عُنُقَهُ جِيدُ دُمْيَةٍ، فِي صَفَاءِ الْفِضَّةِ، مُعْتَدِلُ الْخَلْقِ، بَادِنٌ مُتَمَاسِكٌ، سَوَاءُ الْبَطْنِ وَالصَّدْرِ، عَرِيضُ الصَّدْرِ،

بَعِيدُ مَا بَيْنَ الْمَنْكِبَيْنِ، ضَخْمُ الْكَرَادِيسِ، أَنْوَرُ الْمُتَجَرَّدِ، مَوْصُولُ مَا بَيْنَ اللَّبَّةِ وَالسُّرَّةِ بِشَعَرٍ يَجْرِي كَالْخَطِّ، عَارِي الثَّدْيَيْنِ وَالْبَطْنِ مِمَّا سِوَى ذَلِكَ، أَشْعَرُ الذِّرَاعَيْنِ، وَالْمَنْكِبَيْنِ، وَأَعَالِي الصَّدْرِ، طَوِيلُ الزَّنْدَيْنِ، رَحْبُ الرَّاحَةِ، شَثْنُ الْكَفَّيْنِ وَالْقَدَمَيْنِ، سَائِلُ الْأَطْرَافِ أَوْ قَالَ: شَائِلُ الْأَطْرَافِ خَمْصَانُ الْأَخْمَصَيْنِ، مَسِيحُ الْقَدَمَيْنِ، يَنْبُو عَنْهُمَا الْمَاءُ، إِذَا زَالَ، زَالَ قَلِعًا، يَخْطُو تَكَفِّيًا، وَيَمْشِي هَوْنًا، ذَرِيعُ الْمِشْيَةِ، إِذَا مَشَى كَأَنَّمَا يَنْحَطُّ مِنْ صَبَبٍ، وَإِذَا الْتَفَتَ الْتَفَتَ جَمِيعًا، خَافِضُ الطَّرْفِ، نَظَرُهُ إِلَى الْأَرْضِ، أَطْوَلُ مِنْ نَظَرِهِ إِلَى السَّمَاءِ، جُلُّ نَظَرِهِ الْمُلَاحَظَةُ، يَسُوقُ أَصْحَابَهُ، وَيَبْدَأُ مَنْ لَقِيَ بِالسَّلَامِ

Hind Ibn Abi Hālah ﷺ said regarding the description of the Prophet ﷺ: "He had great qualities and attributes; others held him in high esteem. His blessed face shone like the full moon. He was slightly taller than a man of middle height, but shorter than a tall person. His blessed head was moderately large. His blessed hair was slightly curled. If his hair parted naturally in the middle he left it so; otherwise he did not habitually make an effort to part his hair in the middle. The Messenger of Allah ﷺ had a luminous complexion, and a wide forehead. He had dense and fine eyebrows. His eyebrows were separate and did not meet in the middle. A vein between them used to expand when he became angry. His nose was aquiline and had a

light and lustre on it. His beard was full and dense, and his pupils were dark. His cheeks were full of flesh. The mouth of The Messenger of Allah ﷺ was moderately wide and his teeth had a slight gap between them. A thin line of hair ran from his chest to his navel. His neck was beautiful and thin, like the neck of a statue shaved clean; it was unblemished and shone beautifully like silver. All the parts of his body were of moderate size and fully fleshed. His body was proportionately jointed. His chest and stomach were aligned, his chest was broad and wide, as was the space between his shoulders. His joints were strong and large. When he removed his clothing, his body looked bright and shone with light. Between his chest and navel was a thin line of hair; besides this line neither chest nor stomach were hairy, though hair grew on both shoulders and on the upper portion of his chest. His forearms were long, and his palms were wide. His palms and feet were fully fleshed. His fingers and toes were moderately long. The soles of his feet were a little deep. Because his feet were clean and smooth, water did not remain there but flowed away quickly. When he walked, he lifted his legs with vigour, leaned slightly forward and placed his feet softly on the ground. He walked at a quick pace and took long

steps, never short steps. When he walked, it seemed as though he was descending to a lower place. When he looked at something, he turned his whole body towards it. He had a low gaze, focused more often on the ground than on the sky. His habit was to look at something quickly, not to stare immodestly. While walking, he'd ask his Companions to walk in front, and he himself walked behind. He greeted whomever he met."

As-Suyuti in Jami' As-Sagheer, graded Sound by As-Suyuti and acceptable by Al-Bayhaqi. Others have graded this hadith as Weak.

عَنْ أَبِي هُرَيْرَةَ، قَالَ ﷺ: وَلَا رَأَيْتُ شَيْئًا أَحْسَنَ مِنْ رَسُولِ اللهِ ﷺ كَأَنَّ الشَّمْسَ تَجْرِي فِي وَجْهِهِ، وَمَا رَأَيْتُ أَحَدًا أَسْرَعَ فِي مِشْيَتِهِ مِنْ رَسُولِ اللهِ ﷺ كَأَنَّمَا الْأَرْضُ تُطْوَى لَهُ إِنَّا لَنُجْهِدُ أَنْفُسَنَا وَإِنَّهُ لَغَيْرُ مُكْتَرِثٍ

Abu Hurayrah ﷺ said, "I have never seen anyone more handsome than The Messenger of Allah ﷺ. It was as if the brightness of the sun shone from his face. I never saw anyone walk faster than him; it was as if the earth folded for him. In the span of a few moments he would be here, and then there.

References

We found it difficult to keep pace when we walked with him, and he walked at his normal pace.

Ahmed and Ibn Hibban, graded Sound

عَنْ أَبِي فِرَاسِ رَبِيعَةَ بنِ كَعْبِ الأَسْلَمِى ﷺ، خَادِمِ رسُولِ الله ﷺ، وَمِنْ أَهْلِ الصفة ﷺ، قَالَ: كُنْتُ أَبِيتُ مَعَ رَسُولِ الله ﷺ فَآتِيهِ بِوَضُوئِه، وَحَاجَته فَقَال: سَلْنِي، فَقُلْتُ: أَسْأَلُكَ مُرَافَقَتَك فِي الجنة. فَقَال: أَوَغَيْرَ ذَلكَ؟ قُلْت :هوَ ذَاك، قَالَ: فَأَعِنِي عَلَى نَفْسِكَ بِكَثْرَةِ السجُود

Rabi'ah bin Ka'b Al-Aslami ﷺ (a servant of the Messenger of Allah ﷺ and also one of the people of As-Suffah) said: "I used to spend my nights in the company of The Messenger of Allah ﷺ and used to pour water for his ablutions. One day, he said, 'Ask something of me.' I said: 'I request your companionship in Paradise.' He inquired, 'Is there anything else?' I said, 'That is all.' He said, 'Then help me in your request by prostrating (in Prayer) a lot.'"

Sahih Muslim

عَنْ أَبِي سَعِيدٍ قَالَ قَالَ رَسُولُ اللَّهِ ﷺ أَنَا سَيِّدُ وَلَدِ آدَمَ وَلَا فَخْرَ وَأَنَا أَوَّلُ مَنْ تَنْشَقُّ الْأَرْضُ عَنْهُ يَوْمَ الْقِيَامَةِ وَلَا فَخْرَ وَأَنَا أَوَّلُ شَافِعٍ وَأَوَّلُ مُشَفَّعٍ وَلَا فَخْرَ وَلِوَاءُ الْحَمْدِ بِيَدِي يَوْمَ الْقِيَامَةِ وَلَا فَخْرَ

Abu Sa'id ﷺ reported that The Messenger of Allah ﷺ said: "I am the master of the children of Adam, and it is no boast. I will be the first for whom the earth is split on the Day of Resurrection, and it is no boast. I will be the first to intercede and he whose intercession will be accepted, and it is no boast. The banner of praise will be placed in my hand, and it is no boast."

Ibn Majah, graded Authentic

مُحَمَّدٌ رَسُولُ اللَّهِ

Muhammad is the Messenger of Allah.

The Noble Quran, Surah 48, Al-Fath, Verse 29

أَخْبَرَنَا مُحَمَّدُ بْنُ عَبْدِ الْأَعْلَى، قَالَ حَدَّثَنَا خَالِدٌ، قَالَ حَدَّثَنَا شُعْبَةُ، عَنْ قَتَادَةَ، قَالَ سَمِعْتُ أَنَسًا، يُحَدِّثُ عَنْ أُسَيْدِ بْنِ حُضَيْرٍ، أَنَّ رَجُلاً، مِنَ الْأَنْصَارِ جَاءَ رَسُولَ اللَّهِ ﷺ فَقَالَ أَلَا تَسْتَعْمِلْنِي كَمَا اسْتَعْمَلْتَ فُلَانًا قَالَ " إِنَّكُمْ سَتَلْقَوْنَ بَعْدِي أَثَرَةً فَاصْبِرُوا حَتَّى تَلْقَوْنِي عَلَى الْحَوْضِ

Usaid bin Hudayr ﷺ narrated: "A man from among the Ansar came to the Messenger of Allah ﷺ and said: 'Will you not appoint me (to a position of authority) as you appointed so-and-so?' The Messenger of Allah ﷺ said: 'Some will prefer others over you after I am gone, so be patient until you meet me at the pond (Al-Hawd).'"

An-Nasa'i, graded Authentic

لَعَلَّكَ بَاخِعٌ نَفْسَكَ أَلَّا يَكُونُوا مُؤْمِنِينَ

(O Prophet), are you going to worry yourself to death because they will not believe?

The Noble Quran, Surah 26, Ash-Shu'ara, Verse 3

31

وَأَمَّا بِنِعْمَةِ رَبِّكَ فَحَدِّثْ

And talk about the blessings of your Lord.

The Noble Quran, Surah 93, Ad-Duha, Verse 11

32

فَاصْبِرْ كَمَا صَبَرَ أُولُو الْعَزْمِ مِنَ الرُّسُلِ...

So be patient, (O Muhammad), like those messengers of firm resolve.

The Noble Quran, Surah 46, Al-Ahqaf, Verse 35

33

...وَإِنَّكَ لَتَهْدِي إِلَىٰ صِرَاطٍ مُسْتَقِيمٍ

...And indccd, (O Muhammad), you guide to a straight path.

The Noble Quran, Surah 42, Ash-Shura, Verse 52

Learning Islam should be fun!

If you agree, you'll love our products...